GOD'S
COMFORT
for
HARD TIMES

Randy Petersen

Publications International, Ltd.

Randy Petersen is a writer and church educator from New Jersey with more than 40 books to his credit, including *All About Heaven, Praying Together,* and *Why Me, God?* A prolific creator of church curriculum, he's also a contributor to the *Quest Study Bible*, the *Revell Bible Dictionary*, and the iLumina Bible software.

Cover photo: Goodshoot

Louis Weber, CEO
Publications International, Ltd.
7373 North Cicero Avenue
Lincolnwood, Illinois 60712

ISBN-13: 978-1-4127-5288-6
ISBN-10: 1-4127-5288-4

Manufactured in China.

8 7 6 5 4 3 2 1

CONTENTS

CHAPTER 1
In the Pit

No matter how low we go,
God will hear our cry and
whisper his love.

The details of the scene are etched in her memory. Gail
had just heated up a couple of pieces of her famous peach
pie to enjoy with her husband. She remembers sitting at
the kitchen table, grateful for the quiet since the children
had been tucked into bed. But Mac had been a bit too
quiet. Gail talked too much, as she did sometimes to fill a
silence. She reported all the trivial events of her day, but
in the pauses there was just the clink of Mac's fork on the
plate. If only she could have frozen time in that moment.
If only she had never heard what came next.

"I need to move out," he had said. "I'm leaving."

With those seven words, Gail's life changed forever.
She thought she had been living a storybook life, packed
with love and blessing, but suddenly the prince had
turned into a troll. Previously she had complained about
traffic jams and bad weather, but she soon discovered
what hard times were really about.

For the first few months, Gail was in a fog: putting on a smile for the kids, telling herself that Mac was just going through a phase. He'd be back, she just knew it. And when he returned, he could fix that leaky pipe in the upstairs bathroom, he could pay those bills, he could take little Megan to the orthodontist. Of course, Mac never did come back, and those things didn't get done. Gail slowly realized she was parenting for two, and that was tough. There had been a certain flexibility when both she and Mac were around. Working late, going to a meeting, dashing to the store—these were easy when Mac was there to watch the children. No more.

She started throwing things. Pillows mostly, but also a bedroom lamp and once a bucket of fried chicken. She found an old set of plates and had a field day—literally. In a field near her home, she smashed the ceramics inside a beat-up trash can. Venting helped, but there was always more anger. Her kids were never in danger, but she did snap at them more often; it didn't take much to set her off. Increasingly, she felt like that trash can, full of broken shards of what used to be a life.

The thing about hard times is that everything seems to make everything else harder. Her short fuse nearly got her fired from her job, and it probably cost her a pay raise. As she sank into depression, she had trouble focusing at work, and of course she couldn't work nights and weekends to meet deadlines. In her marketing firm, Gail had gone from a rising young star to dead weight. She found herself getting colds and the flu more often, exhausting all her sick time in just two months. After that, they docked her pay.

Money was already tight. Mac sent an occasional check, which Gail used for the children's clothes and school supplies, but it was never enough. She fell behind paying bills. She was running up the only credit card she had in her own name. Friends told her she needed to get a good lawyer, but how would she pay? Meanwhile, the drip in the bathroom was causing water damage in the downstairs walls. She didn't know how to fix it, and she couldn't afford to hire anyone who did.

*The thing about hard times
is that everything seems to make
everything else harder.*

Her kids were getting irritable, too, and that made it harder to handle them. One night the youngest one chirped, "Daddy would let us have ice cream," and Gail lashed back, "Well, Daddy isn't here right now because he decided he didn't want to be with us anymore. So I'm all you've got, and you'll have to just shut up and deal with it." That made everyone cry, and Gail figured that she had just flunked Parenting 101.

She went to sleep early that night, right after the kids went to bed. She slept until noon the next day. She dozed through the alarm, through the tumult of children bouncing around her, through the phone ringing and the concerned message of her assistant from the office: "Um, we had a meeting. Went over the numbers. Hope everything is all right. Call me."

Gail finally got up and padded into the kitchen to fix breakfast—er, lunch. The children were in the other room enjoying the rare treat of weekday TV. Watching the coffee drip-drip-drip into the pot, Gail thought, *Look at me—I'm ruining my life and everyone else's. This is just too hard. I can't do this.* Then she sat down at the kitchen table—the same place this whole mess had started—and she did something she hadn't done in a long time. She began to pray.

THE PROBLEM WITH PROBLEMS

You can probably relate to Gail, at least a little bit. Even if you've never faced the challenges of divorce or single parenting, you might have lost a job or sustained a debilitating illness or injury. Perhaps you're caring for a loved one who is suffering. Maybe your family has been touched by alcoholism or drug addiction. Or are you mourning the loss of someone you cherished? Any of these crises can send you into the kind of tailspin Gail experienced.

The problem with hard times is that the problems pile up. "If it ain't one thing, it's another," as they say. Your crisis may start with a single event, but soon you're struggling with several different challenges. For instance, you might be going through the agonizing process of finding a new home for your elderly parents. It's a deeply emotional transition, especially if they need more medical care than you can offer. However, not only are you dealing with your parents' tender emotions, you might also be wondering how to pay for an adequate facility as well as fighting with your siblings about the details. Emotional issues can quickly become economic, and they may threaten the peace of all your relationships.

In this way, one problem can soon become two or three, and these situations feed into one another: If you lose your job, you'll have financial worries, but you might also take a hit to your self-esteem, and all of this could do damage to your marriage. In turn, that might make it harder to focus on finding or keeping a new job, so the problems continue. It's as if you have fallen into a pit, and instead of a rope you find a shovel. As you desperately struggle to climb out, you just keep digging your way deeper into the pit. Sometimes it seems that everything you try just makes things worse.

THE CYCLE OF WOE

You might be involved in a "cycle of woe," in which different types of problems spin you around. First, there's the basic **sorrow,** or grief, over the situation. First and foremost, Gail missed her marriage. Obviously her feelings for her husband changed with his betrayal, but she still felt the loss of that once-happy relationship. She was sad that it was gone.

The same thing might be said for a number of other crises. If you have been diagnosed with a serious illness, it's natural to grieve the loss of your good health. If your teenagers get in trouble at school, you'll feel sad about this—and you'll also feel concerned or angry or determined to discipline them. But the first, basic response is simply sadness.

Most crisis situations then involve **practicalities.** This is where your life gets complicated. You'd like to have a good cry, venting the sorrow that's welling up within you, but you can't. You have to go and meet with the school principal. Or you have to haggle with your health insurance provider. If you're mourning the death of someone close to you, you might have to make arrangements for the funeral or burial. As Gail faced the difficulty of single parenting, her to-do list doubled. Even though you're emotionally wounded, it's hard to take time to convalesce because now there are even more things to do.

Generally these practicalities cost you time and/or money, two resources you never have enough of, even when things are going well. When hard times occur, you suddenly have to squeeze new responsibilities into your schedule, or you have to find extra cash in your account. Not easy to do. Since time and money are limited resources, something will have to give. So you spend less time at your job or with your family or for your own restoration, which jeopardizes your employment, relationships, or health. You might have to tighten your budget, squeezing out luxuries first and then necessities. Maybe you get behind on bill payments or get caught up in a credit trap. Nowadays many folks are losing their homes because they can't meet the mortgage payments. That creates a whole new set of practical problems.

Relationships get strained in these hard times. Husbands and wives often fight about money. When your schedule tightens up, your family may resent the fact that you have less time for them. You may have upset coworkers because you're not pulling your weight, friends who miss the time they used to spend with you, or parents who are tired of lending you money. Not only are the practicalities stretching you, your sorrow is turning you into someone who isn't very good company. That's not your fault—you have emotional stuff to work through—but it can make you angry or depressed or dependent. The situation gets worse when a whole family is dealing with the same grief. When *everyone* becomes angry or depressed or dependent, relationships fray... or explode.

Ironically, these are the times when you need relationships the most. You need people to support you, to encourage you, to understand that you're having a crisis. Your friends and family need to know that you may be a bit erratic during this time, and they should give you the benefit of the doubt. When this happens, the downward spiral can be slowed, stopped, or reversed. Yet all too often, negative reactions from others can make your hard times worse.

These are the times when you need relationships the most.

Of course, all of this creates **stress.** If you're emotionally wounded, worried about having enough time or money, and bickering with those around you, it will wear on you. Mentally, you'll be distracted, which may cause you to make bad decisions that worsen your situation. A single mom like Gail might fall in love too soon, hoping a new man will solve all her problems—and that would probably just reopen old wounds. Physically, you'll find your heart beating faster, your blood pressure up. You'll be more susceptible to disease. You'll get tired faster. This is when people get sick and miss workdays.

So just when you need to think smarter and work harder, you're sabotaged by stress, which cycles back upon those practicalities, creating even more challenges than you had before. If it ain't one thing, it's another.

As the problems mount, even the most devout believers can go through severe **questioning.** How could God let this happen? Doesn't he love me anymore? I thought he promised me an "abundant life"—so how can I hurt so much? Did I do something to make him hate me? Some people begin to blame God for their problems, and as a result, they turn away from him. It's hard to go to church, to read the Bible, to pray. In these trying times, God seems far away, so these faith-based activities seem empty, even painful. In a way, these people are spiritually sulking. They are getting back at God by removing themselves from him.

For many who go through this questioning period, a deep sense of **guilt** takes over. Maybe they feel ashamed for being so angry with God—shouldn't they have more faith? Maybe they begin to see ways that they brought their misfortune upon themselves—they must have deserved this, they figure. Or maybe they disparage themselves for not climbing out of the pit sooner—if they had any gumption, wouldn't they be over this by now?

The questioning and feelings of guilt add to the cycle of woe. Without the anchor of faith, people find themselves drifting. They don't know what their priorities should be. They lose their sense of purpose.

DRAW ME NEARER

But not everyone drifts away. Some move *toward* God in their times of difficulty. They may not understand what God is doing or why he's doing it, and they haven't processed all the theological issues. They don't have the answers to all their questions, but they know they're lost without a connection to God. They may even be miffed at him. Maybe they storm up to God's throne and say, "God, I'm upset with you right now. Where have you been? I'm suffering here, and you don't seem to care! But here I am, talking to you. What do you have to say for yourself?"

Granted, most people aren't that bold before the Creator of the universe, but everything in Scripture indicates that God doesn't mind when you tell him how you feel. He would much rather see you coming toward him with a complaint than running away with a grudge.

In these trying times, you need more than answers: You need love. You need a love that has the power to lift you out of the pit. You need a love that can transform you, using your difficulties to make you stronger. You need a love that whispers encouragement even when your situation seems hopeless.

"I waited patiently for the Lord," the psalmist wrote, "he inclined to me and heard my cry. He drew me up from the desolate pit, out of the miry bog, and set my feet upon a rock, making my steps secure" (Psalm 40:1–2). And that's just what you need, isn't it? A foothold. Some kind of traction so you can take steps forward and out of this mess you've fallen into.

When we left Gail, she was sitting at the kitchen table with a cup of joe, half the day gone already. She saw her situation as clear as day. She had fallen and couldn't get up—not without some outside help. And so Gail grabbed a hazy memory from her youth, bowing her head and folding her hands like a Sunday school student, and she haltingly entered the presence of the living God.

"I'm a mess, God. I'm sure you know that more than I do, but you have to do something, not just for me, but for my kids. I don't want to bring them down with me. I'm not asking for a miracle; I just need the strength to get through each day. Well, maybe that *is* asking for a miracle, but that's what you do, isn't it? Help me, please. Help this family. We need you."

She wasn't sure what to expect. Would the lights flicker? Would lightning strike? Would she get a phone call that would change everything? As she set about preparing lunch, Gail wondered how God could fix things for her family. What tiny miracles were needed to get them back on their feet?

There was no sudden visitation, no angelic vision, but she slowly gained the energy to do something she should have done a long time ago. She took the kids out for ice cream.

A Prayer for Hard Times

Lord God,

There are times when I have no clue what to do, but I know something has to be done. I get so far down I don't know which way is up. I can blame everyone around me for betraying, mistreating, or neglecting me, but I know I've also contributed to the mess I'm in. And I'm pretty good at blaming myself, too.

So, what are we going to do about this? I've tried everything I can think of, and I just seem to make things worse. Do you have some secret solution to my problems? Dare I use the word miracle? Because I think I've come to the end of myself, and all I can say is, "Help! Please help!"

Maybe this is where you wanted me all along, completely relying on you. I know our relationship hasn't always been smooth, but I'm here now, and I need you in my life more than ever. Help, please help.

And I won't forget to thank you when you do. Amen.

A Scripture for Hard Times

Where can I go from your Spirit?
Where can I flee from your presence?
If I go up to the heavens, you are there;
if I make my bed in the depths, you are there.
If I rise on the wings of the dawn,
if I settle on the far side of the sea,
even there your hand will guide me,
your right hand will hold me fast.
If I say, "Surely the darkness will hide me
and the light become night around me,"
even the darkness will not be dark to you;
the night will shine like the day,
for darkness is as light to you.

PSALM 139:7–12 NIV

CHAPTER 2
God Sees Us

When we're stuck in the desert, he lets us know we're not forgotten.

It's not one of the nicest stories in the Bible, but it carries a deep message of hope. Some Bible passages just aren't for kids, and Genesis 16 would fall into that category. By modern standards, the behavior of Abraham and Sarah seems wrong, out of character. Apparently these giants of faith took a misstep, and a slave girl named Hagar got trampled.

God had promised that Abraham (then known as Abram) would have descendants as numerous as the stars in the sky. One problem: Abraham was now an old man and childless. Even more to the point, his wife Sarah (Sarai) was also aged, clearly too old to bear children. Yet God had made this promise, and Sarah figured out a way to fulfill it.

Hagar was her handmaid, an Egyptian slave. According to Middle Eastern customs of the time, a wife could give her handmaid to her husband for the purpose of bearing children; this was how rich men built their clans.

If you're slamming on the brakes now—good. There are several bothersome issues in this story, including slavery. Why did they have a slave at all? Was Hagar forced to consort with Abraham and bear this child? Did she have any say in the matter? We could spend quite a while digging into the history and theology of this account, but let's not. The Genesis text shows no outrage over these points, depicting Abraham and Sarah as people of their time, doing things that their society allowed. Despite that, Sarah's plan wasn't what God had in mind.

At first it seemed to work just fine. Hagar got pregnant, and this apparently raised her status a little. She was no longer just Sarah's handmaid but a second "wife" to Abraham. Ancient culture put great value on a woman's ability to conceive, so this became a point of leverage for the servant girl. While Sarah was feeling the shame of barrenness, Hagar had the glory of pregnancy. It's hard to blame Hagar for exulting in her new role. As a slave she would have been little more than a household appliance: fetching water, fixing meals, doing whatever her mistress demanded. Now she was nearly part of the family, the mother of the heir. We're told that Hagar treated Sarah with "contempt." Was that in the form of unkind words, a haughty way of carrying herself, or just self-pampering? "I'd love to brush your hair, Sarah, but the baby just kicked, so I'd better take it easy." Was this contempt intended by Hagar or imagined by an over-sensitive Sarah? Maybe both.

Whatever form it took, this attitude drove Sarah to a breaking point. "May the wrong done to me be on you!" she cried to her husband. "I gave my slave-girl to your embrace, and when she saw that she had conceived, she looked on me with contempt. May the Lord judge between you and me!" (Genesis 16:5)

Abraham had to be thinking, *Just how is this my fault? It was your idea in the first place.* But he didn't argue with his distressed wife. "Your slave-girl is in your power; do to her as you please," he replied (verse 6).

Perhaps Abraham had seen Hagar as a second wife, pampering her and treating her as part of the family. If so, that stopped. Sarah began treating Hagar "harshly," no doubt reminding her that she was only a slave after all. This treatment pushed Hagar to her limit, and she ran away. She headed toward Egypt, her homeland.

JOURNEY TO NOWHERE

A brief geography lesson: Abraham was a nomadic rancher in Canaan, which had a semiarid climate. In the foothills, there was grass for animals to graze, but as you went south, toward Egypt, everything became drier. A few springs flowed at certain places in the desert, providing occasional oases. Still, the journey from Canaan to Egypt was long and difficult. For a pregnant woman, it would be downright dangerous. Food and drink would be scarce along the way, and there was always the possibility of attack by wild animals or bandits.

Did Hagar plan her escape, or did she just take off one day after Sarah's latest tirade? Was she well-equipped for the journey? Probably not. Did Abraham and Sarah go after her? Apparently not. But God did.

"The angel of the Lord found her by a spring of water in the wilderness, the spring on the way to Shur [which was near Egypt]. And he said, 'Hagar, slave-girl of Sarai, where have you come from and where are you going?'

"She said, 'I am running away from my mistress Sarai'" (verses 7–8).

We don't know exactly how far she had traveled. She was just "on the way," or along the road. (Clues in the text suggest a journey of 5 to 7 days.) It's no surprise that she was at a roadside spring; that was her sustenance. There was a well that drew water from that spring, and she was sitting by it. Perhaps she considered herself lucky to find that water source and wasn't sure where the next one was. Stuck in the middle of nowhere with her unborn child, she seemed to have no idea what would come next. Talk about hard times! She had been up and down emotionally in recent months: a second wife, a rival, an abused slave—and that doesn't even take into account the effect of her mother-to-be hormones. She had been pampered and then punished. At this point, physically, she was at the end of her rope, trying to eat for two in a landscape that couldn't provide for one. Tired, confused, and afraid, Hagar received a visit from God's angel.

When we, like Hagar, go through hard times, it's easy to lose sight of the big picture.

The angel's question is a good one to remember in our own times of fear and confusion. Where have we come from, and where are we going? Of course, it can be answered in immediate terms—"I'm coming home from work and going to the store"—but what happens when we zoom out to look at the bigger picture? Where are we going *in life*? And what *life-shaping experiences* have we come from? When we, like Hagar, go through hard times, it's easy to lose sight of the big picture. We're plodding from day to day with no sense of a long-range future. Similarly, we get cut off from our previous identity, seeing ourselves only as "the person with problems." Yet there are many influences that have made us who we are, and in our hard times we can draw on a wealth of resources from the past. "Where have you come from, and where are you going?" Get the larger vision.

That's exactly what the angel does for Hagar—he zooms out. "The angel of the Lord said to her, 'Return to your mistress, and submit to her.' The angel of the Lord also said to her, 'I will so greatly multiply your offspring that they cannot be counted for multitude'" (verses 9–10). This was essentially the same promise God had given Abraham, and now he thought enough of Hagar to promise it to her.

A bit of patching up needed to happen in the short term. Hagar had to go back and undo some damage—that would certainly be difficult for her. Like the Prodigal Son in Jesus' parable, she had no idea how she would be received, but the Lord was telling her flat out: Go back and be a slave again. Yet there was a larger vision here, almost too large to comprehend. Hagar had a future. She would be the mother of countless people. In the immediate future this meant that she would give birth—"Now you have conceived and shall bear a son." This in itself was great news for Hagar, who must have feared the effects of her rigorous journey on her child. She was told to name him Ishmael, which means, "God hears"—"For the Lord has given heed to your affliction" (verse 11).

We don't know what kind of relationship Hagar had with God before this. She had probably been taught about the gods of Egypt, but surely Abraham and Sarah had told her about their God, the one who had spoken to Abraham. Even if she didn't know much about him, she must have cried out to him in this time of affliction because he was *giving heed.* The Hebrew word for that is *shema,* to hear. And not just to hear, but to respond. God had heard her prayer. Stuck in the desert between a tumultuous past and a hazy future, she had desperately launched a prayer—and it worked! This God cared about her situation and was offering her guidance and a promise.

She wasn't sure what to call this God who came to her rescue, the God who paid attention to her plight. So she called him "The God Who Sees Me." As a memorial of this life-giving, soul-saving moment, she gave the well a name: *The Well of the Living One Who Sees Me.*

WHAT'S IN A NAME?

What name do you have for God? Is he the Creator, the Righteous One, the Judge of the Living and the Dead? Is he the One From Whom All Blessings Flow? Then what happens when the blessings stop flowing? Is he the One Who Makes Sure People Get What They Deserve? If so, it is no wonder you feel guilty for the misfortunes you have had.

There are many names for God in Scripture, and ferreting them out is a rewarding study. While he has revealed many different aspects of his character, people tend to focus on one or two at a time. In fact, you may be struggling with some of these revealed aspects right now, as you figure out how the God Who Is Love can also be the All-Powerful God and still let such awful things happen to you. We'll sort through some of that later, but for now, as you try to deal with your times of affliction, it might be best simply to take a page from Hagar's book and worship The Living One Who Sees Me.

When you think you're all alone, when you're afraid that everyone has abandoned you, when it seems that you could just wither away and no one would know the difference—remember that God saw a pregnant slave girl by a well on a desert road, he heard her cries for help, and he assured her of his great plans for her. That Living One is still living today, and he sees you. He hears your cry for help. He pays attention to your needs.

It was not far from Hagar's well that the Lord spoke to Moses. After killing an Egyptian slave master, Moses had escaped in the opposite direction, out of Egypt, and was tending sheep in the Sinai Peninsula. At the burning bush, God announced to Moses, "I have observed the misery of my people who are in Egypt; I have heard their cry on account of their taskmasters. Indeed, I know their sufferings, and I have come down to deliver them from the Egyptians, and to bring them up out of that land to a good and broad land, a land flowing with milk and honey" (Exodus 3:7–8). Once again, God revealed himself as One Who Sees, One Who Hears, One Who Pays

Attention. He had big plans for Moses, which involved freeing his people from slavery and leading them toward that "good and broad land."

Often our troubles "enslave" us. We feel that our options are limited; we can't do what we please. If only we were healthy, if only we were free of this addiction, if only we had a solid relationship, if only we had a new job— *then* we could really live. And of course we toil under various "taskmasters," some human and some institutional. There are bills to pay, children to rear, neuroses to cope with. All of these pressures "crack the whip" in one way or another. We cry out for relief.

It may not be a burning bush that brings you before the living God. It may not be an angel delivering the divine message. Maybe it's a trusted friend, or a Bible verse, or even this book. Or it could be a gentle whisper you hear before you drift off to sleep or as you wait in a checkout line. In any case, receive the message. Draw strength from the words you hear: *God sees your situation. He hears your cries. He knows your suffering.*

SEEING PAST AND FUTURE

❊ ❊ ❊

God doesn't just see the present moment. He also pays attention to where you've come from and where you're going.

He knows everything that you have been through, every ingredient that makes you the person you are today: every supportive teacher, every strict parent, every sour love affair, every loyal friend. He knows your strengths and weaknesses, the temptations that taunt you, the memories that haunt you. "For he knows how we were made," the psalmist says, "he remembers that we are dust" (Psalm 103:14). He was there when the first human was scooped up and sculpted from the soil. He sets high standards for you, but he understands your dusty passions. His mercies are new every morning. He sees where you've been, and he offers forgiveness, redemption, comfort, and healing.

He also sees your future. Your difficulties have narrowed your vision to the challenges of each day, but he sees far beyond that. He sees the person you will become. Testing makes a person stronger, and he sees how you will grow through these hard times. He sees the people you will influence, the character you will show. Now you see your faith hanging by a thread, but he sees a battle-tested soul that can have a powerful impact on others in the future.

During his own hard times in prison, the Apostle Paul wrote to encourage one beloved congregation, assuring them that he was "confident of this, that he who began a good work in you will carry it on to completion until the day of Christ Jesus" (Philippians 1:6 NIV). We are works in progress. Our Creator is still sculpting us.

Mrs. Geng was an odd little lady who taught eighth-grade math. She also had a keen eye. In one of her lower-level classes, one student kept acting out. Day after day, Joe would disrupt the class and get sent to the principal's office. In all of his classes, his grades were dreadful and dropping fast, but Mrs. Geng saw something in Joe. She told the principal, "Put him in my top class. He's not stupid. He can do the work."

The principal thought she was crazy. It was ludicrous to put this problem child with the top students. He would just disrupt that class, wouldn't he? But Mrs. Geng kept pressing the matter until the principal gave in.

The move transformed Joe. It turned out he was actually good at math, and he embraced the challenge of competing with the smart kids—not by picking fights but by passing tests. Most importantly, perhaps, someone finally saw him as a valuable person in the school: a teacher who accepted his past and believed in his future.

That's what the Lord does for us. "Where have you been? Where are you going?" he asks us. And if we listen carefully, we can hear him whispering about a far better future ahead for us.

A Prayer for Hard Times

*O Living One Who Sees Me, thank you for
paying attention. Often I feel invisible, as if
my problems are hidden from everyone. I long
for someone to understand me, to recognize
my situation, to see that I need a helping
hand or a kind word. But I can rest in the
knowledge that you see me. You know exactly
what I'm up against and precisely what I need.
You listen to my cries for help and hear every
syllable of my prayers.*

*And that's why I pray to you now. Lord, please
take a good look at my circumstances and
step in to help me. Encourage me, enliven me,
and empower me through your grace. Amen.*

A Scripture for Hard Times

The Lord looks down from heaven;
he sees all humankind.
From where he sits enthroned he watches
all the inhabitants of the earth—
he who fashions the hearts of them all,
and observes all their deeds....
Truly the eye of the Lord is on those who fear him,
on those who hope in his steadfast love,
to deliver their soul from death,
and to keep them alive in famine.

PSALM 33:13–15,18–19

CHAPTER 3
God Is With Us

Massive miracles are rare,
but his quiet presence helps us grow.

A storm blew up as Jesus and his disciples were crossing the Sea of Galilee. This must have been a real bone-rattler because the disciples were terrified, even though several of them were experienced fishermen. They had often sailed this body of water, but this wind was unusually treacherous. "The waves beat into the boat, so that the boat was already being swamped" (Mark 4:37).

Jesus was asleep. He had spent the day navigating crowds, so he left the seafaring to his friends and sacked out in the back of the boat. (Archaeologists have found fishing vessels from that period with room for about a dozen people and an open area at one end where they might stash their catch ... or a tired rabbi might curl up for a nap.)

As the tempest raged, the disciples were furiously pulling in sails and manning oars, with the fishermen barking orders to the nonfishermen. Some were bailing water. Then someone realized that their best resource might be their sleeping leader. "They woke him up and said to him, 'Teacher, do you not care that we are perishing?'" (verse 38).

Freeze the action, mid-storm, and put yourself in the story. Or perhaps put the story in yourself. What hurricane-force winds have been blowing you around? Have you been swamped by a sudden storm? Has the normal journey of your life been made treacherous by forces you can't control? Do you feel you're bailing water like crazy but still sinking?

If so, then maybe you've asked the same question the disciples shouted on the Sea of Galilee: "Do you not care that we are perishing?" Shockingly, the Lord seems to be sleeping through the crisis, in his own dreamworld somewhere, oblivious to your needs. It seems that he just doesn't care.

The biblical story has a happy ending: Jesus "woke up and rebuked the wind, and said to the sea, 'Peace! Be still!' Then the wind ceased, and there was a dead calm. He said to them, 'Why are you afraid? Have you still no faith?' And they were filled with great awe and said to one another, 'Who then is this, that even the wind and the sea obey him?'" (verses 39–41).

Wouldn't it be nice if he did that with your problems, just waved his hand and made them go away? The truth is, he can do that, and sometimes he does. There are accounts of miraculous restorations, but the Lord usually chooses to work in a less obvious fashion.

FINDING ANSWERS IN THE QUESTIONS

✻ ✻ ✻

We can learn a great deal by answering the unanswered questions in this story. First, the disciples ask Jesus, *"Do you not care that we are perishing?"* At first blush, the question seems nonsensical. *Anyone* would care about this situation, especially the teacher who challenged others to "love your neighbor as yourself." Yet, in their tumult, they scold Jesus for sleeping through the storm, just as we might complain that God dozes off when we need him most.

Does he care? Absolutely. "I have loved you with an everlasting love," God once announced to a nation in crisis (Jeremiah 31:3). He cares about us in an everlasting way, which extends beyond the challenges of this life. His love lasts beyond our current crisis, beyond our death, into the reaches of eternity. Does he care about our earthly existence, about our physical well-being? Yes, but that's not all he cares about. He cares even more about our souls, our faith, our growth. Is that why he slept through the disciples' panic? He created a teachable moment that would last forever.

That brings us to the double question Jesus asked: *"Why are you afraid? Have you still no faith?"* This sounds like a harsh rebuke until we realize that faith formation was at the heart of Jesus' relationship with these people. He often chided them for having "little faith," though he once said that only the tiniest amount of faith—a mustard-seed's worth—would be sufficient to move mountains. Through events like this, he was building their faith.

Let's put ourselves in the disciples' sandals and try to answer the following questions. *Why be afraid?* Oh, it might have something to do with the 40-foot wave sweeping over a 20-foot boat. We're in danger here! This is exactly the kind of situation fear was invented for! *Don't we have faith?* Of course we do, but this is different. We believe that Jesus can enthrall a crowd and even heal people, but this is nature we're up against.

He cares about us in an everlasting way, extending beyond the challenges of this life.

A father once came to Jesus seeking healing for his demon-possessed boy: "'If you are able to do anything, have pity on us and help us.' Jesus said to him, 'If you are able!—All things can be done for the one who believes.' Immediately the father of the child cried out, 'I believe; help my unbelief!'" (Mark 9:22–24). You might say that's what Jesus was doing with his disciples over his three-year stint with them: Taking their mustard seeds of faith and challenging their unbelief. Bit by bit, they gained appreciation for his power. First he healed people with his touch. Then he healed others long-distance. Here he did something the disciples couldn't fathom—he stopped a storm. He was expanding their faith at each step.

Even now, we set limits on what we think the Lord will do for us. Sometimes our situations seem so overwhelming that we can't imagine how God could make it better. He would have to change everything; he would have to transform *us*. And maybe that's the whole point. Yes, he does care about us, deeply, but God is more interested in building our faith than in fixing our problems.

The third unanswered question from our story is the disciples' open-mouthed gasp: *"Who then is this, that even the wind and the sea obey him?"* Understandably, they were awed by this display of power. Their buddy, Jesus, just told the weather what to do. Obviously he was more than a carpenter, more than a teacher, more than a healer. They had to expand their vision of him.

When we ask God to address the storms of our lives, we need to ask the same question, but we need to view the answer in a different way—not on a large scale, but a small one. When we go to the Creator for help, who are we dealing with? The all-powerful deity who can snap his fingers and part the sea? Yes, by definition, he is that. But perhaps we need to *contract* our vision and begin to see him more as a counselor, a friend.

"Do not fear, for I am with you," the Lord told his people while they were in captivity, "do not be afraid, for I am your God; I will strengthen you, I will help you, I will uphold you with my victorious right hand" (Isaiah 41:10).

He is with you! That's the faith that conquers fear. It's interesting that this passage avoids the language of stilling storms. Sure, the Creator can stop armies dead in their tracks, but here the promise is subtler. He will strengthen, help, and uphold us. He will be involved in our lives, ever deepening our relationship with him and giving us the strength to get through the storms.

Who is this Lord we worship? A storm-stopper, yes, but also a fellow passenger. Maybe the most remarkable thing about that trip across the Sea of Galilee happened before the sky even started clouding up: The Lord was in the boat with them! Whatever storms they had to weather, the Son of God would weather them, too. Remember, one title given to Jesus at birth was Emmanuel, which means, "God is with us" (Matthew 1:23).

THE SOUND OF SILENCE

That might be the single most encouraging thing for you to hear as you struggle through your hard times: *God is with you.* When you feel alone and helpless, you can find solace in the fact that God not only sees your situation but he also sits there with you. Whether or not he works a miracle to change the course of nature, it is miracle enough for him to share your sorrow. Sometimes he gives you more than a solution; he gives you himself.

Elijah found himself depressed and alone in a desert cave. He had won a huge victory over the false prophets who were corrupting his country, but that didn't seem to change anything. The queen was still out to kill him, so he fled south. Another runaway, like Hagar and Moses, he landed in the arid Sinai. Elijah was downright suicidal.

Sometimes he gives you more than a solution; he gives you himself.

"'What are you doing here, Elijah?' the Lord asked, and Elijah lit into a tirade, 'I have been very zealous for the Lord, the God of hosts; for the Israelites have forsaken your covenant, thrown down your altars, and killed your prophets with the sword. I alone am left, and they are seeking my life, to take it away'" (1 Kings 19:9–10). Days earlier this prophet had called fire from heaven, but now he was whining about the futility of it all. He had done everything right, but everything went wrong. Maybe you know the feeling.

Elijah was told to leave the cave and stand on the mountain, "For the Lord is about to pass by." There the prophet witnessed three natural spectacles, first "a great wind, so strong that it was splitting mountains and breaking rocks in pieces," but we're told that "the Lord was not in the wind." Then came an earthquake and a fire, but the Lord was "not in" these displays of nature either. What followed was a "sheer silence" (verses 11–13). Other translations call it a "gentle whisper" or a "still, small voice."

We know that God can work mighty miracles, but they're rare—that's why we call them miracles. Most of the time he works in sheer silence. He speaks in a gentle whisper. His still, small voice reminds us that he is there even when no one else is.

If a situation is to be transformed,
it's because God is in the middle of it.

In Elijah's case, the voice gave him work to do. The pity party was over—this prophet needed to anoint a couple of kings and his successor. Elijah's faithfulness wasn't futile after all. He was just going through a bad time.

Sometimes we wonder how to pray for others when we're not sure what the best outcome is. We can pray for healing for the sick and hope for the discouraged, but do we dare pray that somebody will get a job, a house, a raise? Some believers have learned to pray that God will "be with" the folks on their prayer list. In one sense, that's quite vague. Isn't God always with us? Yes, but that's where any solution starts. If a situation is to be transformed, it's because God is in the middle of it. He will bring comfort and motivation, clarity and peace as needed. There's probably nothing wrong with praying for wind, earthquakes, or fire—or any mighty deeds that would instantly change a situation—but we get on God's page when we pray for his redemptive presence to be felt in the "sheer silence."

DOES GOD HIDE?

Even the most faithful believers go through periods when God seems absent. Try as they might, they don't hear his gentle whisper. This can be an agonizing time, but it can also lead to growth.

There's a story of a mother who was teaching her teenage daughter to cook. They had teamed up in the kitchen for weeks, and the daughter was slowly gaining confidence, but she still double-checked with her mom on every decision. "Use this pan for the stir-fry?" she'd ask. The time came for her to cook a meal for the family by herself. Wisely, the mom decided to leave for the afternoon; she had a "meeting scheduled." The daughter was terrified. "What if I have questions?"

"You will, of course," Mom replied, "but do your best to answer them. You can always go back to the cookbook if you need to."

"Can I call your cell?"

"You can leave a message, but I'll have to turn it off for the meeting."

What Mom didn't say was that her "meeting" was with her neighbor across the street. They sipped coffee together all afternoon, sitting by the window. "If my house goes up in flames, I want to be the first to see it," Mom quipped. She was kind of nervous about this experience, too.

In a way, the daughter felt abandoned, but she did her best. She tried calling her mother for one detail, but then hung up when she saw the answer in the cookbook. All in all, dinner turned out to be a success. The meat was a bit tough and the potatoes a little lumpy, but the string beans had a great new collection of spices on them. Everything was edible, and no one got sick. It was a major step forward for this young chef.

And maybe that's the sort of thing God does with us sometimes, perching "across the street" to let us cope with things on our own. This is a hard idea to accept, and it may need to be mulled over for some time. Paul told the Athenians, "Indeed he is not far from each one of us" (Acts 17:27), and that's certainly true, but might there be times when his whisper is quieter than usual so we have to listen more closely? Can we grow closer to him in the silence?

OUT OF THE FRYING PAN...

❋ ❋ ❋

When the Jews were taken as captives to Babylon, there were four young men selected for important positions in the Babylonian civil service—Daniel and three others: Shadrach, Meshach, and Abednego. It was difficult for them to remain faithful to their Jewish ways in this foreign land. The problem came to a head when the Babylonian king set up a golden statue and held a massive dedication service, demanding that all the leaders worship the idol. This violated the first two of the Ten Commandments, so these young Jewish men refused. Daniel is not mentioned in this story, but the three others—Shadrach, Meshach, and Abednego—took their stand and suffered the consequences.

"But if you do not worship," the king warned them, "you shall immediately be thrown into a furnace of blazing fire, and who is the god that will deliver you out of my hands?" (Daniel 3:15)

The young men responded, "If our God whom we serve is able to deliver us from the furnace of blazing fire and out of your hand, O king, let him deliver us. But if not, be it known to you, O king, that we will not serve your gods and we will not worship the golden statue that you have set up" (verses 17–18).

We expect biblical heroes to stand up to pagan braggarts and boldly claim God's victory. We want them to say: "God *will* deliver us." But notice the amazing lack of certainty here. They knew God *could* save them from the fire, but *would* he? They had seen their nation overrun by these arrogant Babylonians. The priests had assumed that the Jerusalem temple would ward off any attackers, but the temple itself was looted. Apparently God had his purposes, but it was tough to see the nation fall to this foreign army. We can't blame these three men for thinking that the time for miracles might be over. Maybe God had given up on them. Still, they would be faithful. Obedience was important, whether or not it led to a divine rescue.

The king was "so filled with rage... that his face was distorted. He ordered the furnace heated up seven times more than was customary, and ordered some of the strongest guards in his army to bind Shadrach, Meshach, and Abednego and to throw them into the furnace of blazing fire" (verses 19–20). The overheated fire even killed some of the guards who put the three Jews in it.

Then the king saw something strange: "Was it not three men that we threw bound into the fire?...But I see four men unbound, walking in the middle of the fire, and they are not hurt; and the fourth has the appearance of a god" (verses 24–25).

A miracle was in the making. Pause here for a moment and imprint this image on your mind. Take this snapshot with you: Three faithful believers in the flames, suffering unjustly, but then a fourth appears—God stands with his people in the fire.

The miracle concludes with the three young men stepping out of the furnace unharmed—unsinged! The baffled king declared that people needed to start respecting the God of Shadrach, Meshach, and Abednego. Anyone who didn't would be "torn limb from limb" (verse 29).

Will God work such a miracle for you? Maybe, maybe not. If you have felt abandoned by God lately, it may be difficult to imagine that he'll step into your turmoil. But you might be surprised. It often happens that, after a long, bleak period, we look back and see that he was there all along, standing with us in the flames.

A Scripture for Hard Times

Take me out of the net that is hidden for me, for you are my refuge. Into your hand I commit my spirit; you have redeemed me, O Lord, faithful God.... I will exult and rejoice in your steadfast love, because you have seen my affliction; you have taken heed of my adversities, and have not delivered me into the hand of the enemy; you have set my feet in a broad place.
Be gracious to me, O Lord, for I am in distress.

PSALM 31:4–9

A Prayer for Hard Times

Loving Lord,
Thank you for caring for me. Sometimes I forget
how much you love me and how you've shown it
time and again. I'm sorry for doubting your love,
but I ask you to help me trust you. Whatever it is
inside me that has to grow in order to trust you
more, help it grow. I know my faith isn't all it
should be, but I want it to get stronger.
Please "help my unbelief."

I do believe that you have the power to transform
my situation. Those "storms" that threaten me
today can be gone with a wave of your hand.
I also know that you have the power to transform
me. I am ready for that to happen. Use these
storms to develop me, to draw me closer,
ever closer to you.

In your mighty name, Amen.

CHAPTER 4
God's Greatness and Goodness

He has the power to transform our troubles.

Newly married, Harry was looking for a better-paying job. He found one 400 miles away from where he and his bride, Darlene, lived. So they moved away from the church where they met, leaving all those friends behind. Buying a beautiful old farmhouse in the country, they began their new life together.

Their idyllic existence soon soured. They found a church in their new area but attended only sporadically. Both of them felt lonely, missing their friends from their old church. Then Harry was laid off from his job. Unfamiliar with the rural environment, he had trouble getting a new one. Their beautiful house now seemed like a ball and chain, keeping them tethered to the area. Both of them sought part-time employment—odd jobs, anything to make ends meet—but it just wasn't working. When Harry was offered a position with a company in another state, he had to take it, even though it required him to drive several hours each Monday morning, stay with a friend all week, and commute home on Friday nights. This helped them pay some bills, but it was difficult for the newlyweds. Darlene was even lonelier during the week, and their weekends were often filled with spats and disappointed silence. Clearly their relationship was wearing thin.

Then Harry learned that Darlene was having an affair. He kicked her out of the house; times had been hard for both of them, but this was a low point. Now, Harry not only had no real home, but no one to come home to. He felt jinxed, as if he would never be happy again. Over the next few months, Harry began to find reasons to drive back to his home church, where he had first met Darlene, and where he still had a pack of friends. Their kind words served to bolster his spirits somewhat, but he especially relished their prayers. Only God could turn this around.

The turnaround began slowly with the easy sale of the farmhouse and an amicable split with Darlene. For a year, Harry did a similar weekly commute between his distant job and his home church, now sleeping weekends in the guest room of a church friend. His wounded emotions were salved by the love of the congregation. Eventually, Harry found a job near the church, and he even began to date again. Today he remembers the pit he was in, and he gives God all the credit for pulling him out. It didn't happen overnight, but it happened.

In this book we've been examining how God works, being careful to avoid reckless promises. If we're expecting prayer to work like some magic wand, instantly turning all our scars into stars, we may be disappointed. But maybe we're being *too* careful. The truth is that God has the awesome power to change things, and often he steps into our lives in surprising ways; let's not sell him short. He can transform us and others, turning our hard times into good times. His sense of timing is different from ours, and he often works miracles that are different from those we ask for, but he loves to help us and heal us.

God has the awesome power to change things.

In Harry's case, the restoration was slow and steady, mediated by a caring community. Step by step things got better for him. (The healing process moved forward for Darlene as well, but that's another book.) And yet there are numerous stories of immediate and miraculous help— a job offer that comes when an unemployed, single mom has just written her last check; a just-evicted tenant who happens to meet a friend of a friend who's looking for a house-sitter; a doctor looking at test results and exclaiming, "The cancer's just *gone*—I've never seen anything like this." God has the power to amaze us.

GO AHEAD—ASK

In the days of the prophet Isaiah, the nation of Judah
was being threatened by two bordering countries. Isaiah
brought a divine message to Ahaz, the king of Judah,
telling him not to worry. The threat would not amount
to anything; God said, "It shall not come to pass" (Isaiah
7:7). The Lord invited Ahaz to ask for a sign to prove this,
but Ahaz refused.

"I will not ask, and I will not put the Lord to the test,"
the king insisted (verse 12). This seems like religious pos-
turing on his part, since he wasn't a very righteous king.
Apparently he was in the middle of battle preparations; he
was finding his own way through the mess, and he wasn't
looking for a bailout, thank you very much.

Get the picture here: God was saying, "Let me show
you what I can do," and the king said, "No, I've got it cov-
ered." No wonder Isaiah sighed, "Is it too little for you to
weary mortals, that you weary my God also?" (verse 13).

Sometimes we do the same thing. In our hard times,
God stands ready to help us. He wants us to ask for his
aid. But maybe we're trying to fix things ourselves, or
maybe we just don't want to seem too religious. It could
be that we're afraid to ask for a specific miracle because,
well, how would we explain it if it doesn't happen? "Ask
me!" God begs us. "See what I can do."

Ironically, the refusal of King Ahaz created a mess for his son and successor, Hezekiah. In answer to the local threat, Ahaz made an alliance with an up-and-coming empire to the east—Assyria. Could they come over and knock off these two pesky border countries? Well, they did that—and more. A generation later, the massive Assyrian army was parked outside Jerusalem, threatening to level the town if Hezekiah didn't surrender. The Assyrian commander openly mocked the God of Judah, secure in his assumption that no one, human or divine, could withstand this military juggernaut.

But Hezekiah prayed about it: "Save us, I pray you, from his hand, so that all the kingdoms of the earth may know that you, O Lord, are God alone" (2 Kings 19:19). And the Lord did save them. The siege was delayed as the Assyrian commander was suddenly called away on other business, and then the angel of the Lord attacked the Assyrian camp, striking down 185,000 soldiers.

Biblical history is full of accounts of military struggles in which the Lord showed his power against overwhelming odds. It's as if God is a secret weapon that neutralizes conventional battle forces. The psalmist sings, "Some take pride in chariots, and some in horses, but our pride is in the name of the Lord our God" (Psalm 20:7).

The prophet Elisha displayed that trust when he faced a trying time of his own. Through his prophetic gift, he had predicted the battle tactics of the Aramean (Syrian) army and warned the Israelites. This perturbed the king of Aram, who sent an army to capture Elisha. One morning the prophet's assistant looked out and saw the enemy army surrounding the city. Elisha consoled him: "Do not be afraid, for there are more with us than there are with them" (2 Kings 6:16). After the prophet asked God to open the assistant's eyes, he looked again, "and he saw; the mountain was full of horses and chariots of fire all around Elisha" (verse 17).

There's another snapshot for you. When you feel surrounded by your problems, blink a few times and see the reality of the situation. "Do not be afraid, for there are more with us than there are with them." The forces of your God are surrounding all the forces that surround you.

UNIMAGINABLE

Scripture presents the message loud and clear. "For nothing will be impossible with God," the angel tells Mary, the mother-to-be (Luke 1:37). Jesus confirmed, "For God all things are possible" (Matthew 19:26). The Lord even boasted to one prophet, "See, I am the Lord, the God of all flesh. Is anything too hard for me?" (Jeremiah 32:27).

Psalm 46 says, "God is our refuge and strength, a very present help in trouble. Therefore we will not fear, though the earth should change, though the mountains shake in the heart of the sea; though its waters roar and foam, though the mountains tremble with its tumult" (verses 1–3). The biblical poets loved to trumpet the Creator's power over the created order. The earth can be a frightful place; tempests and earthquakes often make people feel helpless, but the Lord is even more powerful. And he is always ready to help the faithful.

In our world there are more powers that can shake us. We face corporate mergers that lay off workers by the thousands, economic downturns that make it hard to put food on the table, unscrupulous moneylenders jacking up interest rates, and an oil industry that makes a tank of gas a luxury item. We deal with kids who won't behave, lovers who break our hearts, and leaders who let us down. Our own bodies are breaking down, and our willpower weakens daily. A buffet table of temptation is laid out for us, and we find ourselves damaging our own lives with lusts and addictions. Can God be our refuge from those forces? Can he deliver us from those enemies?

Yes, he can.

When the Apostle John was writing about the spiritual conflicts in our society, he said, "The one who is in you is greater than the one who is in the world" (1 John 4:4). At one level we can take that as assurance that God is greater than the devil, but the implication is even larger. Of all the devilish forces in the world—greed, lust, inhumanity, selfishness—none of them can defeat God. That's what

Paul refers to when he announces that we are "more than conquerors" because of the Lord's love. "For I am convinced that neither death, nor life, nor angels, nor rulers, nor things present, nor things to come, nor powers, nor height, nor depth, nor anything else in all creation, will be able to separate us from the love of God in Christ Jesus our Lord" (Romans 8:38–39). That's quite a list, and it certainly includes any corporation or health-care plan that's causing woe.

Take note of what is promised there. None of those forces will be able to *separate us from God's love.* We might still lose a job; we might still go bankrupt; we might have to change our long-held plans. And yet through all of that we remain connected to God's love. Our Creator will lovingly provide for us, working within us to do powerful things. That's the ultimate goal here—not the country house or the vacation in Aruba, but a purposeful life lived in God's love and power.

When Paul prayed for his friends in the Ephesian church, he didn't ask for material wealth or even freedom from persecution. He prayed that they would be "strengthened in [their] inner being," and that they would be "rooted and grounded in love" (Ephesians 3:16–17). He closed that prayer with an inspiring benediction: "Now to him who by the power at work within us is able to accomplish abundantly far more than all we can ask or imagine, to him be glory" (verses 20–21). The power of

God is indeed great—beyond our imagination. Best of all, that power is at work *within us.*

GREAT TO GOOD

❋ ❋ ❋

Maybe that's where you've heard enough, though. It's nice to see that promise for devout believers, that God's power within them will get them through hard times, but will that also work for you? You may feel that you have brought your hard times upon yourself. Bad choices or lack of discipline may have put you where you are. Maybe you blame yourself for some grievous sin, and you feel you have to pay the consequences. God may work his greatness through other people, but you're afraid you don't qualify.

There's good news: God isn't just great—he is good. He's not just *able* to use his mighty power to combat your problems, he is *willing* to show kindness to you, even when you don't deserve it. We read in Psalm 103:8–13:

> The Lord is merciful and gracious,
> slow to anger and abounding in steadfast love.
> He will not always accuse,
> nor will he keep his anger forever.
> He does not deal with us according to our sins,
> nor repay us according to our iniquities.

For as the heavens are high above the earth,
    so great is his steadfast love toward those who
    fear him;
as far as the east is from the west,
    so far he removes our transgressions from us.
As a father has compassion for his children,
    so the Lord has compassion for those who
    fear him.

Even if you're right in thinking that you have caused your own difficulties, that's old news as far as the Lord is concerned. He is more than ready to let bygones be bygones. He's eager to remove those sins "as far as the east is from the west" and start fresh.

The Lord your Redeemer invites you to "forget the shame of your youth" (Isaiah 54:4) and listen to his call. "For a brief moment I abandoned you, but with great compassion I will gather you . . . with everlasting love I will have compassion on you" (verses 7–8). That was originally a message to his people in captivity, but it extends to all captive souls who want a new life.

Hear another word from Isaiah: "Comfort, O comfort my people, says your God. Speak tenderly to Jerusalem, and cry to her that she has served her term, that her penalty is paid" (Isaiah 40:1–2). Our God is great in power, good in love, and he offers you a pathway back to a vibrant life in love with him.

A CITY IN RUINS

❋ ❋ ❋

I will never forget the morning of September 16, 2001.
Five days earlier, the United States was stunned by a ter-
rorist attack and two major structures in New York City
were still smoldering. The nation was in a somber mood.
All week we had seen the images of destruction, the
ruins of a once-prosperous section of town. The following Sunday, I was teaching an adult Sunday school class,
continuing a series on the Old Testament prophets. The
scheduled text was Lamentations.

"How lonely sits the city that was once full of people!"
the book begins (Lamentations 1:1). It was an all-too-
appropriate study for this time of national mourning.

Jeremiah wrote the book of Lamentations after the
Babylonians had swept into Jerusalem, razing buildings,
looting the temple, demolishing the landscape, and cap-
turing many of its citizens. The city lay in ruins. Verse
after verse laments the destruction, expressing remorse
over the spiritual rebellion that brought on this disaster.

My soul is bereft of peace;
  I have forgotten what happiness is;
so I say, "Gone is my glory,
  and all that I had hoped for from the Lord."
LAMENTATIONS 3:17–18

Then, in the middle of this chapter, verses 21–23, Jeremiah sounds a strange note of redemption:

> But this I call to mind,
>   and therefore I have hope:
> The steadfast love of the Lord never ceases,
>   his mercies never come to an end;
> they are new every morning;
>   great is your faithfulness.

The Lord is faithful even when we aren't. Verses 25–26 and 31–32 illustrate that day by day he shows us new kindnesses:

> The Lord is good to those who wait for him,
>   to the soul that seeks him.
> It is good that one should wait quietly
>   for the salvation of the Lord. . . .
> For the Lord will not
>   reject forever.
> Although he causes grief, he will have compassion
>   according to the abundance of his steadfast love.

As you slog through your own "ruins," mourning your missteps and railing against the forces that caused this, let your soul ease into quietness. Seek the Lord in the midst of this mess. Wait to see how he will transform both you and this situation. Take comfort in both the greatness and goodness of your God.

A Prayer for Hard Times

Awesome God,

When I encounter obstacles in life, I believe you have the power to break through them.

When I feel I have no more strength to go on, I believe you have the power to carry me.

When I get stopped at every turn, unable to get where I want to go, I believe you have the power to show me a better route.

When I feel lonely and abandoned, I believe you have the power to rally loving friends around me.

When I am wounded by life's experiences, I believe you have the power to nurse me back to health.

When I am headstrong and proud, I believe you have the power to remind me who's boss.

When I am discouraged and defeated, I believe you have the power to lift me up again.

When I come face to face with the reality of my own sin, I believe you have the power to forgive me and bring me into your holy presence.

These things I believe, in your name, Amen.

A Scripture for Hard Times

Why do you say..., "My way is hidden from the Lord,

and my right is disregarded by my God"?

Have you not known? Have you not heard?

The Lord is the everlasting God,

the Creator of the ends of the earth.

He does not faint or grow weary;

his understanding is unsearchable.

He gives power to the faint,

and strengthens the powerless.

Even youths will faint and be weary,

and the young will fall exhausted;

*but those who wait for the Lord shall renew
their strength,*

they shall mount up with wings like eagles,

they shall run and not be weary,

they shall walk and not faint.

ISAIAH 40:27–31

CHAPTER 5
Working Together

❀ ✾ ❀

God really does bring good things out of bad times.

"All things work together for good, you know."

When you're in the middle of hard times, that's the last thing you want to hear, and yet people keep offering it to you. They're good people—well-meaning Christians who want to say the right thing—but it sounds like they're telling you not to grieve, not to feel the pain you feel. They're writing a happy ending for your story before you've even reached chapter two.

Meanwhile you're suffering with a disastrous diagnosis, the death of a loved one, or a marriage in ruins. Your dreams lie in pieces around you, and somebody's telling you that someday you'll look back on this and laugh? No, you're convinced that there's nothing good about this situation. These statements of hope seem like mere denial.

Of course, "working together for good" isn't some phrase from pop psychology; it's a quote from Scripture. The Apostle Paul used it in a letter to the Romans about suffering. It's worth noting that this reference isn't just about suffering persecution for your faith (as other New

Testament passages are), but it's about a general difficulty with all of life. "The whole creation has been groaning," Paul says, and "we groan inwardly while we wait for . . . the redemption of our bodies" (Romans 8:22–23).

Have we been doing any "groaning" lately? Sure we have! We've been bemoaning the decay of our bodies, decrying the hurtful actions of others, even questioning the acts of God. When we're in that spiritual-emotional pit, we don't even know how to pray. The best we can do is to grunt in God's general direction. Fortunately, Paul says, the Holy Spirit prays on our behalf, translating our groans into "sighs too deep for words." The Spirit intercedes for us "according to the will of God" (verses 26–27).

Only after the groaning does Paul say, "We know that all things work together for good for those who love God, who are called according to his purpose" (verse 28). What is this verse saying? Is it really telling us not to feel bad because everything will turn out all right? Is it denying our current pain in light of some rosy scenario for the future?

Taken in context, Romans 8:28 gives us an amazingly gritty analysis of our problems—not escapism but transformation.

First of all, this passage acknowledges that *hard times are normal.* This "groaning" it talks about is the way of the world. In fact, all of creation is playing this waiting game, enduring the struggle of existence as it waits for God's ultimate redemption. So, if you're worried that your present difficulties somehow exclude you from the rest of the human race, guess again. It's tempting to see yourself as an outcast, removed from God's plans, but that's not the story told here. We all share in the challenges of a universe tainted by sin. We all wait for God to turn things around.

Hard times transform us into stronger servants of God.

The second thing we can read into this passage is this: *We don't always know what the best outcome is.* We don't even know what to pray for, so the Holy Spirit takes our groanings and interprets them according to the good things God wants. In the midst of trying situations, we want things to be better, but how? If we're honest with ourselves, we have to admit that the measures we take to improve matters don't always work, and sometimes they backfire. The "perfect job" turns out to be a nightmare. The "dream house" becomes a money pit. Even lottery winners often find their lives wrecked.

Underlying the teaching of Romans 8:28 is a third insight: *Bad things can work together to make something good.* There's a strange alchemy here. In the hands of our loving God, lead and copper turn to gold. The pain and heartache of our lives turn into growth and trust. Hard times transform us into stronger servants of God.

That's what happened to Joseph.

BAD INTENTIONS

❊ ❊ ❊

Favorite son of Jacob, great-grandson of Abraham, young Joseph had a pretty good life to look forward to—until his jealous brothers sold him as a slave to a passing caravan. Some of the brothers wanted to kill him, so maybe he was lucky to be alive. "Count your blessings," some could say, but that might not mean much since he seemed destined for a life of servitude in Egypt.

Joseph rose to the top of the servant corps, but the master's wife had eyes for him. When he refused her advances, she falsely accused him of rape, and he was jailed. Whatever "blessings" he once had, they seemed irrelevant now that he was discarded on a human trash pile.

But once again Joseph rose to the top, becoming the prison trusty. He earned a reputation as an interpreter of dreams as well, explaining the meanings of dreams for two inmates who were also once in the king's service. In keeping with Joseph's interpretation, one of the inmates—Pharaoh's cupbearer—was released and restored to royal service. Joseph had asked the cupbearer to put in a good word for him with the Pharaoh when the dream came to pass. However, years went by. Hope faded. The favorite son had been forgotten, biding his time in misery and squalor.

Then Pharaoh had a strange dream, and the cupbearer remembered how a fellow prisoner, Joseph, interpreted his dreams in jail. Pharaoh sent for Joseph, who dazzled him, not only interpreting the dream but recommending a national plan to deal with what it predicted—an impending famine—and volunteering to lead it. As it turned out, Joseph's able administration helped Egypt deal with the food crisis, saving many from starvation. Even his brothers came south from Canaan seeking food. After playing a few tricks to ensure that they were sorry for mistreating him, Joseph reunited with them.

At the end of the story, Joseph made a statement that still carries weight today, especially in our current discussion: "Even though you intended to do harm to me, God intended it for good, in order to preserve a numerous people, as he is doing today" (Genesis 50:20).

Amazingly, Joseph says that there were two sets of intentions in the same events. His brothers were trying to hurt him, and they succeeded, but God used that situation for his own purposes. We can play a great "What if?" game with this story. What if Joseph was never falsely accused and imprisoned? He would never have met the cupbearer who introduced him to Pharaoh. What if Joseph was never sold as a slave? He would never have been falsely accused and imprisoned. If his brothers had not done this terrible thing to him, he would presumably have remained in Canaan with his doting father—and maybe he and his family would have died in the famine.

Hypothetical musings like that only take you so far. Surely God would have found another way to preserve this family and keep the pledge to their ancestor Abraham. (This is probably the "numerous people" Joseph was talking about, not the Egyptians. Remember that God had promised Abraham that his descendants would be as numerous as the stars in the sky.) But the point is that God had a purpose—a purpose with long-range historical, even eternal implications. He was not going to let the misdeeds of Joseph's brothers thwart his plans. Everything they intended as evil, he transformed into good. The brothers' savage envy, the mistress's lying lust, the master's misplaced vengeance, and perhaps the cupbearer's temporary forgetfulness were all bad things, but God coordinated them to accomplish something good according to his purpose.

You can still trust that God has something better ahead.

You might find this especially comforting if your troubles are at least partly attributable to someone's misbehavior. If your spouse left you or a coworker lied to get your promotion or a con artist stole your life savings, it's clear that their intentions were harmful, but that still doesn't negate the good purposes of God. Like Joseph, you will suffer the pain of their actions, but you can still trust that God has something better ahead.

LOVE LINES

There's still a fourth component of that powerful-but-sometimes-misused promise of Romans 8:28. To whom is this promise delivered? To those "who love God, who are called according to his purpose." Things work together for good *within a relationship of love and commitment.* Don't view this as a payment or reward, as if things will go 50 percent better for you if you love God that much more. No, this simply puts the statement in a personal context. God has a purpose for those who have entered this love relationship with him. And he will keep things moving toward that purpose no matter what negative events occur.

What do we know about God's purposes? When we look at the entire Bible, Old and New Testaments, we find a progression. First it was the establishment of the nation of Israel—that's what we see in Joseph's story, the "numerous people" being "preserved." Then God wanted a loving relationship with Israel, yet it always seemed that he wanted to expand that relationship to include the whole world. This was the point of the incarnation, death, and resurrection of Jesus—to reconcile the whole world with himself, to provide the "redemption" that the whole universe is groaning for.

Where do you fit in? You're in the middle of it! In his letter to the Colossians, Paul uses resolute language to describe his own ministry. His job is to proclaim the "mystery," the secret purpose of God through all the ages. And what is the mystery? "Christ in you, the hope of glory." That relationship is what it's all about. "It is he whom we proclaim . . . so that we may present everyone mature in Christ" (Colossians 1:27–28).

Our maturity—that's the goal. The New Testament is crammed with prayers and hopes that believers would grow more and more like Christ. And how do we grow? More often than not, it's through the challenges of experience.

"My brothers and sisters," wrote James, "whenever you face trials of any kind, consider it nothing but joy, because you know that the testing of your faith produces endurance; and let endurance have its full effect, so that you may be mature and complete, lacking in nothing" (James 1:2–4). In a similar passage in Romans 5, Paul talked about suffering producing endurance, character, and hope (verses 2–5). Elsewhere, Paul said, "I want to know Christ and the power of his resurrection and the sharing of his sufferings" (Philippians 3:10).

In other words, our hard times give us the opportunity to grow closer to Christ. Our character builds. We begin to understand what's most important in life. We learn the value of waiting for what's best. Even more than that, we find a point of connection with Christ, who suffered for us. Our suffering helps us know him better. It helps us to become more like him. That is God's good purpose to which we are "called," according to Romans 8:28.

The very next verse adds that God has chosen us "to be conformed to the image of his Son." More and more, as we work through our difficulties, we are becoming like Jesus. That is the divine purpose.

TEMPERING A TEMPER

Early on, little Andrew had trouble listening to his parents. From the time he could walk, he had a behavior problem. He seemed to get preoccupied with things, and any attempt to lure him from what he was focused on would cause a tantrum. His father, Martin, had attention deficit disorder, so he wondered if that was Andrew's problem, too. Actually, the diagnosis was even more serious: autism.

It was a moderate case but significant enough to require professional testing and an intricate mode of parenting. With intensive work early in Andrew's life, Martin and his wife, Stacy, could possibly rewire some of his brain processes and get him to function more normally. But this was a frustrating task—not what they had bargained for. They were bright, ambitious fast-trackers. Taking the time necessary to parent a special-needs child, well, that wasn't part of the plan. They had to cut back on outside activities, including some church duties. They grew weary and cranky. "What did we do to deserve this?" they wondered. There were times of anger with God and serious self-doubt. They read about the high divorce rate among parents of special-needs children and worried about their relationship. Though they were deeply committed to each other, they feared that this pressure might tear them apart.

Martin soon discovered a difficult truth: He had a bad temper. He had always known that he had a tendency to lash out when he felt that someone was ignorant or obstinate, but it never seemed to be that much of a problem. Until now. Little Andrew pushed all his buttons: Call him and he ignores you; yell and he still ignores you; get in his face, and *maybe* he'll pay attention. The chances of Andrew actually cooperating were minimal. This fueled Martin's rage multiple times a day.

But expressing that rage just made matters worse. Andrew was very good at throwing tantrums, too. If Daddy threw a tantrum, why should he learn anything different? With both of them flying into fits of rage, nothing could get resolved. The more Martin saw himself in his young son, the more he looked for alternatives to his displays of anger. Martin began to learn how to remain calm in frustrating situations. Since Andrew didn't seem to have control over his emotions, he might benefit from a father who did. It was the hardest thing in the world to speak softly while the boy was screaming, but slowly, slowly, Martin learned to do this. He was learning patience.

And one day, he realized that the problem of Andrew's autism had struck at a cutting edge of his own personality.

What better motivation to tame your temper than to do it for your beloved son? As difficult as it was, and would continue to be, Martin found that this crisis was making him a little more like Christ.

If, when he first got the diagnosis, you had told him, "All things work together for good," he would have politely nodded and quickly changed the subject. It's a religious truism, isn't it? A nice idea but not very helpful. But it's truer than we realize. God uses even our most difficult situations to achieve his good purposes, such as crafting us into the mature believers he wants us to be.

A Scripture for Hard Times

Therefore, since we are justified by faith, we have peace with God through our Lord Jesus Christ, through whom we have obtained access to this grace in which we stand; and we boast in our hope of sharing the glory of God. And not only that, but we also boast in our sufferings, knowing that suffering produces endurance, and endurance produces character, and character produces hope, and hope does not disappoint us, because God's love has been poured into our hearts through the Holy Spirit that has been given to us. For while we were still weak, at the right time Christ died for the ungodly.

ROMANS 5:1–6

A Prayer for Hard Times

Lord, I'm groaning through these hard times. I don't understand how this collection of bad ingredients will ever whip up into something "good," but I leave that up to you. Lately I've experienced one negative thing after another. I'd like to keep a positive attitude, but that's becoming very difficult. So I'm just going to leave it in your hands. Take all the bad luck of my life, the cruel intentions of my associates, the blind neglect of my friends, my own ineptitude, and the ordinary difficulties of existing in this fallen world—take it all and start squeezing it into something helpful.

I don't know how you're going to do it, but I'm hanging onto the hope that you will.

Hold me in your love, guide me in your purpose.
Amen.

CHAPTER 6
Our Heavenly Home

Living in God's kingdom, future and present.

There was laughter at Rachel's funeral. Lots of it. One relative after another got up to relate stories about this dear woman, and it seemed that every story had a punch line. Rachel had lived a vivacious life, deeply connected with the lives of her three siblings, husband, and four grown children. Everyone had a tale to tell, and the church rocked that day with the joy of those memories.

Some might call this denial, but it was really a point of acceptance. A year earlier Rachel had been diagnosed with pancreatic cancer, and her family had felt the shock then. The following months were dotted with doctor visits and hospital stays, as well as treatments that could not forestall the spreading disease. People in a dozen churches were praying for Rachel and her family during that difficult time. Those prayers did not lengthen her life, but they may have been responsible for the joyful funeral.

"My mother was always a fearful person," said one son. "She worried about everything—in her life and in the lives of everyone she knew. But here's the thing: When she found out she was dying, it unleashed courage in her that we'd never seen before. She said what had to be said, she did what had to be done, and she prepared Dad and the rest of us for her departure. She didn't seem upset about it; she wasn't afraid. She was going home."

So in that final year, she was able to help her loved ones deal with their grief. They were able to say goodbye to her properly, and at the funeral they could actually celebrate her "graduation" to a new kind of life in the presence of her Lord.

Anticipating the end of his own life, the Apostle Paul wrote about his emotional conflict. "For to me, living is Christ and dying is gain. If I am to live in the flesh, that means fruitful labor for me; and I do not know which I prefer. I am hard pressed between the two: my desire is to depart and be with Christ, for that is far better; but to remain in the flesh is more necessary for you" (Philippians 1:21–24). Obviously he was ready for the end of his earthly life, because that meant seeing his Savior. On the other hand, he could serve that same Savior in his remaining time on earth. It was win-win.

We get the same sense of continuity in the closing words of the best-known psalm, one that's often read at funerals. "Surely goodness and love will follow me all the days of my life, and I will dwell in the house of the Lord forever" (Psalm 23:6 NIV). With the Lord as his shepherd, the psalmist knows his earthly life is full of God's goodness and love, and the long-range picture is more of the same: living with God forever. This is really a rather innovative idea. The early Israelites didn't think much about an afterlife—you died, you went down to The Pit, end of story. But here we have the suggestion of an eternal existence with the Lord. It's much like what Paul told the Philippians. Earthly life allows divine qualities (such as goodness and love) to flow to us and through us, and then we get to live in God's house forever. It's all good.

It does not show any lack of faith to mourn for someone you'll miss.

Does that mean we should banish tears at funerals? Not at all. Grieving over the death of a loved one is natural, even if we believe that we will see them again in heaven. Rachel's funeral was an exception, where her family and friends marked the end of a year-long grieving period with a remarkable expression of joyous release. But physical, earthly death is still a separation, no matter how we interpret it theologically. It does not show any lack of faith to mourn for someone you'll miss, even if you know they're in a better place.

Edna passed away at the age of 102, after living a faithful life. Driving home from the viewing, her family remained rather stoic about her passing. After all, they told each other, she was in heaven with the Lord, this wasn't a loss but a graduation, and other statements to that effect. "This should be a time of rejoicing," someone said.

Then one of Edna's granddaughters spoke up. "Yeah, but I'm sad! I'm going to miss her." There was a kind of release for the rest of the family at that moment, as if everyone exhaled. They had been sort of censoring their sadness in the interest of theological correctness. But they would all miss this great woman. They could feel sad for the parting and still be glad for the passing.

If your current difficulties have to do with a terminal illness or grief over the loss of someone you loved, you can carry all these emotions together. You don't need to edit them. Cry one minute and laugh the next. That's not craziness; that's reality-based faith.

When the believers in one early church became concerned that some of their loved ones were dying before the Lord's return, Paul wrote: "We do not want you to be uninformed, brothers and sisters, about those who have died, so that you may not grieve as others do who have no hope" (1 Thessalonians 4:13). He went on to talk about God's plans to include those departed ones in the second coming.

The point is that we do have hope. We believe that life does not stop at death but continues in God's presence through eternity. This faith can transform the way we look at death—and the way we look at life.

KINGDOM COME

❄ ❄ ❄

In the Lord's Prayer, we recite, "Thy Kingdom come, thy will be done, on earth as it is in heaven." For many of us, that rolls quickly off the tongue, and we don't think about it very much, but what are we really saying?

Jesus often talked about God's kingdom; it was one of his major themes. The tricky thing about this teaching is that the kingdom is hard to pin down. Is it future or present? Yes, it's both. Is it an actual entity or a state of mind? Yes and yes. Is it some ideal out there or is it within reach, within *us?* Yes, to all of the above.

We're left with the assurance that, by definition, God's kingdom exists wherever God is acknowledged as sovereign, where his will is done. We look forward to a future existence in which the whole universe will acknowledge God, but in the meantime the kingdom exists here and there as people do his bidding. The kingdom is as small as a bit of yeast, with just as much potential for growth.

It is significant that Jesus did much of his teaching about the kingdom of God in stories or parables. "The kingdom of God is like this," Jesus would say, and then he'd find some tidbit from daily life to express a huge idea about

God. It's a treasure found in a field, a costly pearl found in the marketplace, farmhands lining up to receive their wages. It's as if the truth can only be fully expressed in experience. God can't be entirely contained in logical explanations. We need stories where we see but don't see, where we get the point—but maybe there's another point, too.

Have you ever thought that maybe you are writing your own parable? Using your life? We keep thinking that the great truths of God are up there, out there, in some heavenly reference book. But the kingdom parables of Jesus show us that God's truth is intimately connected with our lives—fields, markets, and wages. We could add cell phones, video games, and insurance adjustors. The question is, how does God's kingdom come into your life? How is God honored as your ruler?

There are two aspects of the kingdom that keep showing up in Jesus' parables. One is **surprise.** The farmhands get paid equally for different amounts of work. A dishonest accountant gets praised by his boss. The rebellious son is welcomed home with open arms while the loyal son sulks. The prayer of the gangster is heard before the prayer of the preacher. This is an upside-down kingdom. Are you willing to let God surprise you?

The other aspect we might call **now and then.** There is a clear sense in some parables that right now we only have a taste of the divine kingdom that will be fully realized in the future. Some scholars call this idea "Already but Not

Yet." The vanguards of God's kingdom are at work in our world now, but we await fulfillment in a "new heaven and new earth."

Jesus told one story about a farmer who planted wheat in his field, but at night an enemy "sowed weeds among the wheat" (Matthew 13:25). When the crops grew, the mischief was apparent: weeds and wheat growing together. The farmhands asked if they should pull out the weeds, but the farmer replied, "No; for in gathering the weeds you would uproot the wheat along with them. Let both of them grow together until the harvest" (verses 29–30). This is a great picture of life as we know it. Good and evil coexist for the time being. Weeds and wheat grow together, but we believe there will be a future harvest when our sovereign God makes things right.

So back to our question: What are we saying when we pray "Thy kingdom come"? We're asking God to bring the benefits of his future kingdom into the present. Maybe we're asking him to pull a few weeds. But we're also asking him to surprise us with his grace; we're asking him to make himself known within the stories of our daily lives.

One more thing. Prayer always has a "so what?" component to it. We might imagine God hearing our prayers and asking, "Okay, but what are *you* going to do about it?" Sometimes he lets us have a hand in answering our own prayers. So when we ask for his kingdom to come to earth, in a way we're committing ourselves to its coming.

We are honoring God as our ultimate boss. What are you going to do to bring God's kingdom into your life today?

NO MORE TEARS

The Book of Revelation gives us a glorious picture of the end of time: "See, the home of God is among mortals. He will dwell with them as their God; they will be his peoples, and God himself will be with them; he will wipe every tear from their eyes. Death will be no more; mourning and crying and pain will be no more" (21:3–5).

We look forward to that future time when our struggles will be over, but we also pray for some of those joys to come into our world now. We can pray for healing, because we know God will eventually heal us all in the heavenly kingdom. Maybe he'll choose to preview the coming kingdom for us by enacting a miraculous healing in our time. We can pray for God's powerful solutions to our troubles because we know that is what's ahead for us. Our eternal life has begun already. Can we get an advance on our future joys? Can we just bring a bit of heaven to earth? In Revelation the Lord says, "See, I am making all things new" (verse 5). Can this restoration begin to happen on earth as it does in heaven? Absolutely it can. God does this sort of thing often, but he surprises us with when and how.

Earthly life, as you know, can be a struggle. You've been enduring some hard times, but God stands with you in the struggle. Hear his gentle whisper of comfort. Perhaps your current suffering will help you get to know the Lord in a deeper way. Perhaps he can use it to shape you into a more mature believer. He may work a miracle upon your body or spirit to change your current situation, or he may ask you to wait until you enter your heavenly home. There he will personally wipe away your tears.

A Prayer for Hard Times

Eternal God,

I look forward to that future existence in heaven when tears will be wiped away. I can't wait for those bright and glorious days in your presence. I long to see things clearly, to look back and say, "Ah, that's why you let that happen," to look forward to eons of happiness in your kingdom.

My dark days are lightened by that ray of hope. My pain is lessened by the anticipation of ultimate healing. My present difficulties are nothing compared to the great joy I will experience in that world. Bring it on, dear Lord. Come quickly to redeem this world, to make all things new.

In your everlasting love, Amen.

A Scripture for Hard Times

Then I saw a new heaven and a new earth; for the first heaven and the first earth had passed away, and the sea was no more. And I saw the holy city, the new Jerusalem, coming down out of heaven from God, prepared as a bride adorned for her husband. And I heard a loud voice from the throne saying,

"See, the home of God is among mortals.
He will dwell with them as their God;
they will be his peoples,
and God himself will be with them;
he will wipe every tear from their eyes.
Death will be no more;
mourning and crying and pain will be no more,
for the first things have passed away."

And the one who was seated on the throne said,
"See, I am making all things new."

REVELATION 21:1–5